SONIC MEDITATIONS
PAULINE OLIVEROS

Dedicated to the ♀ Ensemble and Amelia Earhart

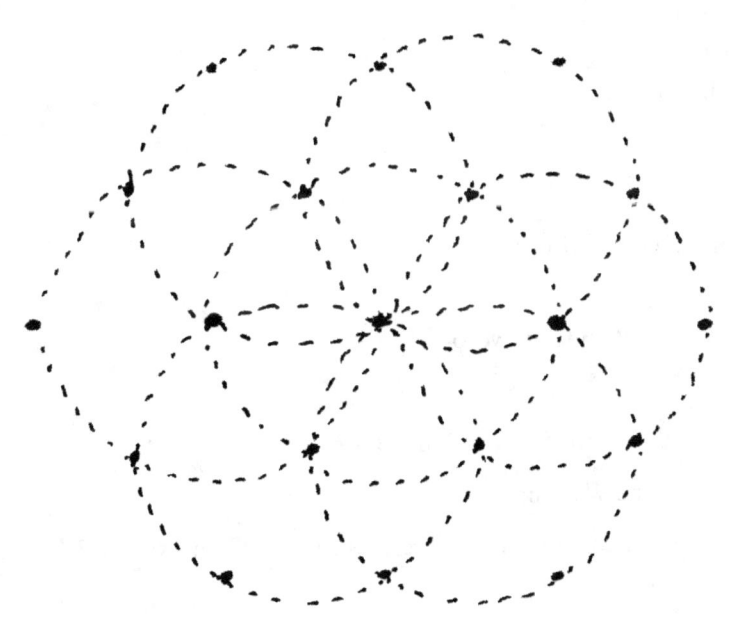

SONIC MEDITATIONS
Pauline Oliveros

Copyright © 2022 PoPandMoM Publications

Foreword: Anne Bourne
After Words: Ed McKeon

Design Team:
Detta Andreana
Zera Bloom
Antonio H. Bovoso
IONE
Norman Lowrey

Cover Design: Detta Andreana

PoPandMoM Logo By Nico Bovoso

Sacred Sound Drawings of Egypt © Anne Bourne

Earth To Sky © Anne Waldman

Photos of Pauline Oliveros at Joshua Tree, Ca., 1971 - Courtesy of Fred Lonidier and Lynn Lonidier

PoPandMoM.org
PO BOX 1956
Kingston, NY 12401

ISBN # 978-1-0880-3853-6
Members ASCAP All rights reserved

First Edition of Sonic Meditations published by Smith Publications 1971

pop & mom

PREFACE

Pauline Oliveros

The meaning of meditation is problematical in that it has accumulated many different associations and a broad range of diverse practices and techniques. It appears often in a religious context, for example Buddhism, Christianity, and Sufism. Its secular counterpart is usually called concentration. Although all meditation, secular and religious, is similar in that it employs attention, awareness, concentration, openness, and repetition, many contrasts among different systems arise. Christian meditation, or contemplation, is usually a dwelling upon specific ideas, such as one's relationship to God, or the pursuit of an activity which is decided upon and directed intellectually. Certain Eastern practices are the opposite, advocating dwelling on emptiness of mind (Nirodha in the Yoga Sutras of Patanjali, "No Mind" in Zen Buddhism). Some methods of meditation encourage mental imagery, others discourage all imagery, some promote the involvement of sense organs using visual, auditory, and somatic forms, others promote the abandonment of sensory modes. Further, there is action versus inaction, feeling versus indifference. In Taoism when action arises, it is spontaneous and natural, while in Confucianism, action is the result of ethics or intellect.

I use the word meditation, rather than concentration, in a secular sense to mean steady attention and steady awareness, for continuous or cyclic periods of time. Any of the above practices or techniques may be employed when appropriate.

While one's attention is focused to a point on something specific, it is possible to remain aware of one's surroundings, one's body, movement of all kinds, and one's mental activity; in other words to remain aware of inner and outer reality simultaneously. Attention is narrow, pointed, and selective. Awareness is broad, diffuse, and inclusive. Both have a tunable range. Attention can be honed to a finer and finer point. Awareness can be expanded until it seems all inclusive.

Attention can intensify awareness. Awareness can support attention. There is attention to awareness; there is awareness of attention.

Attention seems to be equated with mental activity and to be aroused by interest or desire.

Awareness seems to be equated with the body's sensory receptivity. It is activated, or present, during pleasure and pain. Either attention or awareness can interfere with the other depending on the intensity of interest or the intensity of stimulation.

When either attention or awareness predominates or gets out of balance, the other tends to drift or become unconscious: For example, after practicing a difficult passage (or even an easy one) over and over again, with or without success in execution, the musician discovers in some part of the body a cramp which has developed from a faulty playing position. Awareness had been sacrificed for attention and became unconscious, or very low level, returning only with the urgency of the cramping pain. With conscious awareness, the cramp might have been avoided by adjusting the player's relationship to the instrument without sacrificing attention before a cramp could develop. In this case awareness would be supporting attention rather than producing a delayed interference reaction. If the passage was executed successfully, one might consider the cramp a small price to pay or it might not be associated with the activity. (It is also possible to sustain an inner muscular or visceral tension which is not noticeable or visible on the outside, so that the body appears to be in the correct relationship to the instrument.) If the passage was executed unsuccessfully, the faulty position disclosed by the cramp might be blamed and subsequently corrected. In the former case, some musicians who remain unaware for a long time, even years, often end by paying a high price for success.

When such things as severe chronic pains in the back or other parts of the body appear without apparent reason, they may be the result of some small but constantly repeated strain. The symptoms often do not respond to medical treatment, probably because the source of the now chronic ailment is continually repeated as an unconscious habit in association with "correct" habits of playing music. It is therefore most difficult to correct in any way whatever. Besides the misery of such a situation, some musicians are forced to give up playing or singing because of such ailments, but even worse, some never realize the relationship of such illness to inner tension, because the appearance of the playing position seems to be correct and the music may sound right.

The opposite can be true: while awareness of body sensations remains present, attention can lapse or drift attracted by the larger phenomenon of a painful awareness. The musical passage may become automated and sound mechanical, parts or all of it may be interrupted or forgotten as attention is divided or diverted by awareness of the cramp or some other strong sensation.

Attention then refocuses and intensifies awareness.

The proper relationship of attention and awareness can be symbolized by a circle with a dot in the center. (Fig. 1)

The dot represents attention and the circle awareness. In these respective positions both are centered in relation to each other. Awareness can expand without losing its balanced relationship with attention. Attention can be focused, as finely as possible, in any direction and can probe all aspects of awareness without losing its balanced relationship to awareness.

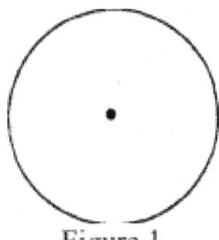

Figure 1

My Sonic Meditations are "sonic" in that sound and hearing, both active and receptive, are the foci of attention and stimuli of awareness, the enhancement and development of aural sensation are among their goals. The synchronization of attention and awareness, that is, keeping them balanced and conscious, is necessary. Also, the synchronization of voluntary and involuntary mental or physical activity is explored. The ear is the primary receptor or instrument, sound, both inner and outer, real and imaginary, is the stimulus of Sonic Meditations.

How and what does one hear? In order to answer this question, the mind must relax, as a muscle must relax, or the appropriate state of expectation must be present in body and mind in order to become receptive to both internal and external stimuli.

A Cup of Tea

Nan-In, a Japanese master during the Meiji era (1868-1912) received a university professor who came to inquire about Zen.

Nan-In served tea. He poured his visitor's cup full, and then kept on pouring. The professor watched the overflow until he could no longer restrain himself. "It is overfull. No more will go in!"

> "Like this cup," Nan-In said, "you are full of your own opinions and speculations. How can I show you Zen unless you first empty your cup?" (Zen Flesh-Zen Bones, Paul Reps, Tuttle)

As a composer I had to empty my cup: I became interested in dwelling on single pitches in my music at the end of the 1950's. There is a very long held note in the cello part of my Variations for Sextet (1959-60). The note lasts approximately half a minute and it is solo. It emerges from a hard attack, together with trumpet, horn and clarinet, with a few low level, evanescent piano harmonics. It is very long in the context of the Variations and other music of its style, which deal with radical shifts in rhythm and timbre. The long cello tone is a very brief meditation, although I was not thinking of it that way at the time. It had at least two functions: 1) It represented a very slow contrasting tempo, within a multiplicity of changing tempi 2) Its harmonic ambiguity increased as it stretched out in time, although the tone itself became an object of interest rather than where it was leading. It signaled my growing interest in timbral shapes and changes, the complementary opposite of chordal or harmonic changes.

Drones of all kinds, such as motors, fluorescent lighting, freeway noise are ever present. The mantra of the electronic age is hum rather than Om. These constant soundings influence everyone, whether consciously or unconsciously. Some adverse effects can occur when the influence is unconsciously received: For example, a musician who unknowingly plays in tune with 60 hz. hum rather than B natural 61.735 in an ensemble. Or an ensemble which does not realize the out-of tuneness caused by the discrepancy between standard musical tuning in reference to A440 and 60 hz. Hum.

I began to seek out drones of all kinds and to listen to them consciously, allowing myself to hear the myriad shifting, changing partials of a constant tone, or of broad and narrow band noise. My subsequent music, both electronic and instrumental, reflected this interest. Whole pieces became single tonal centers or noise bands with characteristic timbral shaping. I was quite satisfied with this work, emotionally and intellectually, although I had apparently abandoned Western harmonic practice.

> *The knowledge of sound can give a person a magical instrument by which to wind and tune and control and help the life of another person to the best advantage. The ancient singers used to experience the effect of their spiritual practices upon themselves first.*

They used to sing one note for about half an hour and study the effect of that same note upon all the different centers of their body: what life current it produced, how it opened the intuitive faculties, how it created enthusiasm, how it gave added energy, how it soothed and how it healed. For them it was not a theory but an experience. (Sufi Inayat Khan, Music, Ashraf Press, Pakistan)

I continued to empty my cup and follow my secular way: My interest and fascination with long tones was centered in attention to the beauty of the subtle shifts in timbre and the ambiguity of an apparently static phenomenon. Why was a tone which went nowhere so seductive? My awareness was adrift.

In 1969 I began to work with dancer, Al Chung Liang Huang, and with him I began the study of Tai Chi Chuan. The work with Huang in this Chinese form of meditation movement involved breath rhythm, synchronized with slow, circular motions of torso, arms and legs. I had been playing and singing with my accordion, slow lingering improvisations on a tonal center. I began to translate the breath rhythms and the slow natural motions of Tai Chi to my solo improvisations. I noticed that I began to feel better physically and mentally, I began to crave more retreat to the calming influence of these drone-like improvisations, from what seemed to be a nervous, frantic music world, full of hasty rehearsals, and constantly noodling performers with uptight vibrations.

By 1970, some other women had joined me to form The ♀ Ensemble, an improvisation group, both vocal and instrumental, devoted to unchanging tonal centers with emphasis on changing partials. After a long period of working together a profound change occurred: rather than manipulating one's voice or instrument in a goal oriented way in order to produce certain effects, we began to allow changes to occur involuntarily, or without conscious effort, while sustaining a sound voluntarily. It is an entirely different mode; and like the professor for whom Nan-In poured continuous tea, opinions and speculations have no place in this activity.

My first conscious recognition of this change resulted in the articulation of "Teach Yourself to Fly," Sonic Meditation I. I say articulated rather than composed because the instructions were transmitted orally many times before being committed to paper.

We could no longer call our activity improvisation.

- Excerpt from original published in Painted Bride Quarterly, Winter 1976

FOREWORD

Anne Bourne

By the time I experienced Pauline Oliveros' transmission of her *Sonic Meditations*, in the *Sangre de Cristo* mountains, in the summer following our meeting in 1994, it was clear to me that she was embracing difference in a new form, on a plane in which each person was of equal distance to the centre point of a sound field. Holding a space of empathic resonance, for the uninitiated singer, the isolated thinker, the multi-lingual, the virtuosic, the deaf conductor, the child no longer bound by ability, the outliers in the room for the first time, contained by trees and glacial erratics, open to perceive complex frequencies of sound in relationship, to compose as a collective in improvisation. It is an experience of love to listen acutely to the subtle, to perceive all human and more-than-human sonics, at the threshold of memory and new beginnings, to sound in waves of self-determining harmonic order.

A sound emerges, within which each unique impulse can be detected, in a balance of attunement and self-expression. In atmospherics and a sonic architecture of time and space, Oliveros creates a shimmer in ephemeral dimensions of activism.

"*Sing Warmly!*" Pauline would provoke, with a twinkle in her eye, in the gentle dialect of a *chorus* from an earlier time. Inhabiting this sound, suddenly these compositions draw from us complex arrays of difference tones, expressed truth, a deep quality of sound that arises out of communal trust, encouraging creative divergence and reach.

The brilliance of Oliveros' scores is the simplicity of her invitation, to lift art; to sense quantum patterns through embodied experience; the possibility of individual and societal wellbeing through expression; in *environmental dialogue* with the internal and all surrounding sound. The quality of listening she proposes may affect all the areas of tension we experience now on this earth, as life presses up against a future where Oliveros imagined... the absence of war.

The Sonic Meditations are a seed bank. Scores encoded with presence. I listen as sound particles move through refracting microtones, to become vibrant, potent and still.

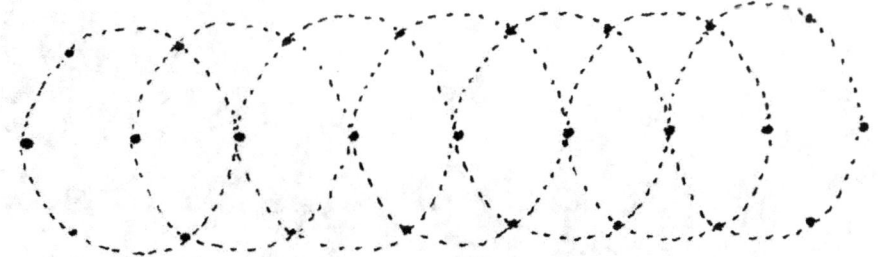

SONIC MEDITATIONS

INTRODUCTION I

Sonic Meditations are intended for group work over a long period of time with regular meetings. No special skills are necessary. Any persons who are willing to commit themselves can participate. The ♀ Ensemble to whom these meditations are dedicated has found that non-verbal meetings intensify the results of these meditations and help provide an atmosphere which is conducive to such activity. With continuous work some of the following becomes possible with Sonic Meditations: heightened states of awareness or expanded consciousness, changes in physiology and psychology from known and unknown tensions to relaxations which gradually become permanent. These changes may represent a tuning of mind and body. The group may develop positive energy which can influence others who are less experienced. Members of the Group may achieve greater awareness and sensitivity to each other. Music is a welcome by-product of this activity.

INTRODUCTION II

Pauline Oliveros has abandoned composition/performance practice as it is usually established today for Sonic Explorations which include everyone who wants to participate. She attempts to erase the subject/object or performer/audience relationship by returning to ancient forms which preclude spectators. She is interested in communication among all forms of life, through Sonic Energy. She is especially interested in the healing power of Sonic Energy and its transmission within groups.

All societies admit the power of music or sound. Attempts to control what is heard in the community are universal. For instance, music in the church has always been limited to particular forms and styles in accordance with the decrees of the Church Fathers. Music in the courts has been controlled through the tastes of patrons. Today Muzak is used to increase or stimulate consumption in merchandising establishments.

Sonic Meditations are an attempt to return the control of sound to the individual alone, and within groups especially for humanitarian purposes; specifically healing. Each Sonic Meditation is a special procedure for the following:

1. Actually making sounds
2. Actively imagining sounds
3. Listening to present sounds
4. Remembering sounds

Because of the special procedures involved, most all of the meditations are available to anyone who wishes to participate regardless, or in spite, of musical training. All that is required is a <u>willing commitment to the given conditions</u>.

Sound making during the meditations is primarily vocal, sometimes hand clapping or other body sounds, sometimes using sound producing objects and instruments.

Sound imagining is encouraged through the use of various questions designed to trigger auditory fantasy. Individuals are then asked to share what was heard inwardly, with members of the group using any means to describe the experience. Conditions given for listening to present sounds are intended to expand awareness of the auditory environment, both within and without of the individual.

Auditory memory is also encouraged by trigger questions with subsequent sharing of these memories in the group. Some of the meditations involve body movement as well. The term meditation is used simply to mean dwelling with or upon an idea, an object, or lack of object without distraction, or divided attention.

Healing can occur in relation to the above activities when 1) individuals feel the common bond with others through a shared experience 2) when one's inner experience is made manifest and accepted by others 3) when one is aware of and in tune with one's surroundings 4) when one's memories, or values, are integrated with the present and understood by others.

In the process a kind of music occurs naturally. Its beauty is not through intention, but is intrinsically the effectiveness of its healing power. This may be felt by the group, and the music relates to the people who make it through participation and sharing, as a stream or river whose waters offer refreshment and cleansing to those who find it.

- I -

Teach Yourself to Fly

Any number of persons sit in a circle facing the center. Illuminate the space with dim blue light. Begin by simply observing your own breathing. Always be an observer. Gradually allow your breathing to become audible. Then gradually introduce your voice. Allow your vocal cords to vibrate in any mode which occurs naturally. Allow the Intensity to increase very slowly. Continue as long as possible naturally, and until all others are quiet, always observing your own breath cycle.

Variation:
Translate voice to an instrument.

- II -

Search for a natural or artificial canyon, forest or deserted municipal quad. Perform Teach Yourself to Fly in this space.

- III -

Pacific Tell

Find your place in a darkened indoor space or a deserted out-of-doors area. Mentally form a sound image. Assume that the magnitude of your concentration on, or the vividness of this sound image will cause one or more of the group to receive this sound image by telepathic transmission. Visualize the person to whom you are sending. Rest after your attempted telepathic transmission by becoming mentally blank. When or if a sound image different from your own forms in your mind, assume that you are receiving from someone else, then make that sound image audible. Rest again by becoming mentally blank or return to your own mental sound image. Continue as long as possible or until all others are quiet.

Telepathic Improvisation

To the musicians with varied or like instruments:

Tuning — each musician in turn sits or stands in front of the audiente for a few minutes. The audience is asked to observe the musician carefully and try to imagine the sound of his or her instrument. The audience is instructed to close eyes and attempt to visualize the musician, then send a sound to the musician by hearing it mentally. The musician waits until he or she receives an impression of a sound mentally, then he or she produces the sound. Members of the audience who have successfully "hit the target" raise their hands as feedback to the musician. After the tuning exercise the musicians distribute themselves throughout the space among the audience members and utilize the following instructions:

1. Play only long sustained tones
2. Play only when you are actually hearing a pitch, or pitches, mentally assume you are either sending or receiving.
3. If you are sending, try to visualize the person to whom you ore sending. If you are receiving, listen for the sound and visualize the sender. The quality and dynamics of the tones you play may be influenced by your feelings, emotional or body sensations, or even impressions of colors, which might come from the audience members. Continue until it seems "time" to stop.

To the observers:

Try mentally to influence the musicians by wishing for one or more of the following elements: (the musicians are instructed to play only long sustained tones)

1. Focus mentally on a specific pitch. If you are sending, visualize the musician to whom you are sending. If you are receiving, listen for the sound which matches yours. Also visualize the musician.
2. Focus mentally on stopping or starting a sound at a particular time.
3. Focus mentally on loudness or softness of tone production.
4. Focus mentally on the quality of the tone.
5. Focus mentally on an emotional character for the tone.
   This meditation is best done in very low illumination, or with eyes closed.

- IV -

Divide into two or more groups. Each group must have a tape recorder and be sound isolated from the other groups. The distance might be small or great, i.e., thousands of miles or light years. Each group then performs Pacific Tell or Telepathic Improvisation, attempting inter-group or interstellar telepathic transmission. A specific time period may be pre-arranged. Each group tape records its own sounds during the telepathic transmission period for later comparison.

Variation:
Instead of working in groups each participant works as an isolated soloist.

- V -

Native

Take a walk at night. Walk so silently that the bottoms of your feet become ears.

- VI -

Sonic Rorschach

With a white or random noise generator, flood a darkened room with white noise for thirty minutes or for much longer. The band width of the white noise should be as broad as the limits of the audio range. A pre-recorded tape or a mechanical source such as an air compressor may be substituted for the generator, if necessary or desired. All participants should be comfortably seated or lying down for the duration of the meditation. Halfway through, introduce one brilliant flash of light or one loud, short pulse. The high intensity flash source could be a photo lamp flash or one pulse of a strobe light. If a sound pulse is substituted for the light flash, it must necessarily be of higher amplitude than the white noise.

Variations:

1. Find a natural source of white noise such as a waterfall or the ocean and go there for this meditation.
2. If the white noise generator is flat, equalize until the source is apparently flat for the human ear.
3. Do this meditation with a different band width represented in subsequent meditations such as one octave at 5k to 10khz.

- VII -
Removing the Demon or Getting Your Rocks Off

Sit in a circle with persons facing in and out alternately. If the number in the group is odd, seat the left over person in the center. Each person except the center person has a pair of resonant rocks. Begin the meditation by establishing mentally a tempo as slow as possible.

Each person begins independently to strike the rocks together full force maintaining the imagined tempo. When enough energy is present, shout a premeditated word. Once selected the word remains the same. The shout is free of the established tempo, and may occur one or more times during the meditation. The center person is without rocks and selects a word, phrase or sentence to say or intone repeatedly either silently or audibly for the duration of the meditation.

Variations:

1. Persons without rocks may sound the circle and follow the some instructions as the center person, independently.

2. Persons may repeat mentally, or actually, one body movement as slowly as possible. One body movement may be simple or very complicated as long as it is continuous and can be repeated exactly as a cycle. Kinetic participants could include the shout or the repeated word, phrase or sentence.

3. Do this meditation in an outdoor environment. Move slowly away from the circle. Move anywhere in the environment but keep in audible contact with at least one other person. Gradually return to the beginning circle.

- VIII -
Environmental Dialogue

Each person finds a place to be, either near to or distant from the others, either indoors or out-of-doors. Begin the meditation by observing your own breathing. As you become aware of sounds from the environment, gradually begin to reinforce the pitch of the sound source. Reinforce either vocally, mentally or with an instrument. If you lose touch with the source, wait quietly for another. Reinforce means to strengthen or sustain. If the pitch of the sound source is out of your range, then reinforce it mentally.

Environmental Dialogue For The New Hampshire Festival Orchestra

To Mary and Tom Nee

On Lake Winnipesaukee, at sunup or sundown, players of the orchestra are dispersed heterogeneously in small groups, in boats all over the lake. Players begin by observing your own breathing. As you become aware of sounds in the environment, gradually begin to reinforce the pitch of the sound source or its resonance. If you become louder than the source, diminuendo until you can hear It again. If the source disappears listen quietly for another. If the source is intermittant your pitch reinforcement may be continuous until the source stops. Aural awareness of the source is necessary at all times even though your reinforcement may be momentarily louder. Reinforcement is distinctly different than imitation. Only strengthen or sustain pitch. Allow the boats to drift unless guidance past obstacles or away from shore becomes necessary.

The Flaming Indian

For Gerald Shapiro and Margot Blum

Tape record a selected environment alone or with a group. Place the microphone carefully in one location. Do the environmental dialogue mentally while you are recording. Reinforce everything you hear mentally. When the meditation is complete, make a translation of the environmental dialogue in the following way: Reinforce the pitches of the recorded sounds with vocal, instrumental, electronic or a combination of these sources. The resulting translation may exist in one or more channels as the translated sounds only or a combination of the translation and original dialogue. A new dialogue is then performed in the same or a different environment with the recorded translation and a soloist or a group, either vocal, instrumental or electronic or any combination. The live dialogue should include the sounds of the live environment as well as the recorded translation.

- IX -

The Greeting

Informed persons should begin the greeting at least half-an-hour or more before a scheduled meeting or program.

After you are seated and comfortable, allow a tone to come into mind. Keep returning your attention to this same tone. Every time a person or persons enter this space, greet them by singing the tone, as you were greeted when you entered this space. Continue this meditation until all are present.

Have you ever heard the sound of an iceberg melting?

Begin this meditation with the greeting meditation (IX). At the designated time for all persons to be present, begin an eight to fifteen minute imperceptible dimming of the house lights down to as dark as possible. When the lights are about halfway down begin the flood of white noise at the threshold of audibility. Slowly make an imperceptible crescendo to a pre-determined sound level, safe for human ears. Approximately twenty minutes later introduce one brilliant light flash. After an hour from the beginning has passed, begin projections on the walls of colorful mandalas, patterns resembling the aurora borealis, or simply colors of the spectrum. The light intensity of these projections should be no greater than the threshold of visibility or just noticeable. These may continue for approximately thirty minutes. Thirty minutes before the white noise ends the space should be illuminated by white light slowly over about eight minutes from the threshold of visibility to as brilliant as possible. The brillance must exceed normal house lighting and approach the intensity of daylight. The end of the light and sound should be sudden and synchronous. Darkness and silence should be maintained for ten minutes or more, then illuminate the space with dim blue light for continued meditation in silence and finally exit of the participants. The duration of this meditation is approximately two to four hours or more. All adjustments of light and sound intensity should be pre-set and preferably voltage controlled. In order that all present may participate in the meditation, and that activities extraneous to meditation may be avoided. Participants must be comfortable, either sitting or lying down.

Variation:

If multiple speakers are used for the production of white noise, one or two persons per speaker could perform meditation movements such as tai chi in front of the speakers at a distance of two to four feet thus creating sound shadows. The sound shadows could gradually be complemented by visible shadows activated by just noticeable light sources. The duration of this part of the meditation could be approximately thirty to forty minutes and succeed or overlap the just noticeable projected images.

- X -

Sit in a circle with your eyes closed. Begin by observing your own breathing. Gradually form a mental image of one person who is sitting in the circle. Sing a long tone to that person. Then sing the pitch that person is singing. Change your mental image to another person and repeat until you have contacted every person in the circle one or more times.

- XI -

Bowl Gong

Sit in a circle with a Japanese bowl gong in the center. One person, when ready to begin, hands the striker to someone else in the circle. That person strikes the gong. Each person maintains the pitch mentally for as long as possible. If the image is lost, then the person who has lost it, hands the striker to someone else in the circle. This person again activates the gong in order to renew the mental pitch image. Continue as long as possible.

All of these Sonic Meditations are intended to begin with observation of the breath cycle.

PAULINE OLIVEROS

SONIC MEDITATIONS XII - XXV

- XII -

One Word

Choose a word. Listen to it mentally. Slowly and gradually begin to voice this word by allowing each tiny part of it to sound extremely prolonged. Repeat for a long time.

Variations:

1. As above, but increase the speed of each repetition as imperceptibly as possible. Continue beyond the normal pronunciation of the word until the repetitions are as fast as possible. Continue.

2. As variation one but when the top speed has been reached and maintained, reverse the process by slowing down again as imperceptibly as possible until the original utterance returns.

- XIII -

Energy Changes

For Elaine Summers' movement meditation, Energy Changes

Listen to the environment as a drone. Establish contact mentally with all of the continuous external sounds and include all of your own continuous internal sounds, such as blood pressure, heart beat and nervous system. When you feel prepared, or when you are triggered by a random or intermittent sound from the external or internal environment, make any sound you like in one breath, or a cycle of like sounds. When a sound or a cycle of sounds is completed re-establish mental connection with the drone, which you first established before making another sound or cycle of like sounds.

- XIV -

Tumbling Song

Make any vocal sound, but always go downward in pitch from the initial attack. The initial attack may begin at any pitch level. Go downward in a glissando or in discrete steps continuously. Go any distance in range, at any speed, dynamic or quality, but the breath determines the maximum time length of any downward gesture.

- XV -

Zina's Circle

Stand together in a circle, with eyes closed facing the center. One person is designated the transmitter. After observing the breathing cycle, individually, gradually join hands. Then slowly move back so that all arms are stretched out and the size of the circle increased. Next stretch the arms towards center and move in slowly. Finally move back to the normal sized circle, with hands still joined, standing so that arms are relaxed at sides. Return attention to breathing. When the time seems right, the transmitter starts a pulse that travels around the circle, by using the right hand to squeeze the left hand of the person next to her. The squeeze should be quickly and sharply made, to resemble a light jolt of electricity. The squeeze must be passed from left hand to right hand and on to the next person as quickly as possible. The action should become so quick that it happens as a reflex, before the person has time to consciously direct the squeeze.

Simultaneously with the squeeze, each person must shout hah. This shout must come up from the center of the body (somewhere a little below the navel) before passing through the throat.

There must be complete abdominal support for the voice. When the first cycle Is complete, the transmitter waits for a long time to begin the next cycle. When the reaction time around the circle has become extremely short, the transmitter makes the cycles begin closer and closer together until a new transmission coincides with the end of a cycle, then continue trying to speed up the reaction time. If attention and awareness are maintained, the circle depending on its size, should be shouting almost simultaneously.

Variations:

1. Reverse the direction of the pulse using the left hand to transmit and the right hand. to receive.
2. Reverse the direction of each cycle,
3. Each person chooses which direction to send the pulse. The transmitter continues to control the beginning and ending of a cycle.

- XVI -

Begin simultaneously with the others. Sing any pitch. The maximum length of the pitch is determined by the breath. Listen to the group. Locate the center of the group sound spectrum. Sing your pitch again and make a tiny adjustment upward or downward, but tuning toward the center of the sound spectrum. Continue to tune slowly, in tiny increments toward the center of the spectrum. Each time sing a long tone with a complete breath until the whole group is singing the same pitch. Continue to drone on that central pitch for about the same length of time it took to reach the unison. Then begin adjusting or tuning away from the center pitch as the original beginning pitch was.

Variation:

Follow the same instructions but return to the original beginning pitch.

- XVII -

Ear Ly

For Kenneth Gaburo's NMCE

1. Enhance or paraphrase the auditory environment so perfectly that a listener cannot distinguish between the real sounds of the environment and the performed sounds.
2. Become performers by not performing.

- XVIII -

Re Cognition

Listen to a sound until you no longer recognize it.

- XIX -

Lie flat on your back or sit comfortably. Open your eyes widely, then let your eyelids close extremely slowly. Become aware of how your eyelids are closing. When your eyelids are closed, turn your eyes slowly from left to right, around, up and down. Let your eyes rest comfortably in their sockets. Try to be aware of the muscles behind the eyes and of the distance from these muscles to the back of the head. Cover your eyes with your palms and shut out all the light. Become aware of all the sounds in the environment. When you think you have established contact with all of the sounds in the external environment, very gradually, introduce your fingers into your ears or cover them with your palms. Try to shut out all external sound. Listen carefully to the internal sounds of your own body working. After a long time gradually open your ears and include the sounds of the external environment.

- XX -

Your Voice

Think of the sound of your own voice. What is its fundamental pitch? What is its range? What is its quality? What does it express no matter what you might be verbalizing or singing? What was the original sound of your voice before you learned to sound the way you sound now?

- XXI -

What constitutes your musical universe

- XXII -

Think of some familiar sound. Listen to it mentally. Try to find a metaphor for this sound. What are the real and imaginary possible contexts for this sound? How many ways does or could this sound affect you? Or how do you feel about it? What is its effect upon you? How can this sound be described?

As a group meditation, sit in a circle. Find a sound common to all, then ask the above questions one by one. Allow plenty of time between each question. When all of the questions have been asked, the group shares their answers.

Variations:
Try the same meditation with

1. An imaginary sound
2. A live sound
3. A remembered sound

- XXIII -

Pure Noise

Sing the purest tone possible, that is, with the fewest partials, in a comfortable register. Gradually change the quality of this tone to include more and more partials until it approaches or becomes a noise band. Continue as long as possible, going from pure tone to noise band with each breath.

Variation:
Reverse the above process.

- XXIV -

Focus your attention on an external source of constant sound. Imagine alternate sounds while remaining aware of the external source.

- XXV -

Your Name

The Signature Meditation

1. Dwell on your name. Write it down as slowly as possible.
2. Visualize your name as you sign it mentally.
    a) with eyes closed
    b) with eyes open
3. Visualize your name in different kinds of writing, script and printing.
    a) vary the sizes from microscopic to gigantic
    b) vary the colors and backgrounds
    c) vary the dimensions from 2 to 3
4. Visualize or actually sign your name backwards, forwards, upside down, inside out.
    a) with the right hand
    b) with the left hand
    c) with both hands simultaneously mirroring each other

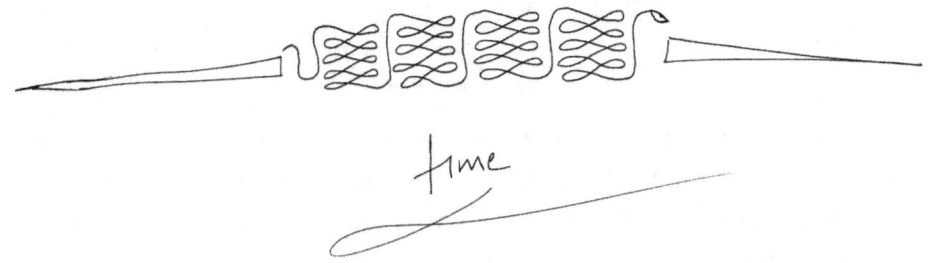

After Words

Ed McKeon

Why re-issue these *Sonic Meditations* 50 years after Pauline Oliveros published her first collection? There are many good reasons, of course: to celebrate her life and work; to mark a seminal moment in the metamorphosis of musical possibilities; to make the texts widely available again; and to provide a key resource for musicians, scholars, artists, activists, and healers. Underpinning these motives lies another, I think. These thoughtful exercises are urgent now—in and beyond the 2020s—in ways that both resemble and differ from the conditions in which they arose. To be concise: *these both are and are not the same words.*

These are not (only) historical documents and they cannot be preserved from time's alteration and aging. Oliveros certainly never treated them that way but incorporated them into her lifelong and continuing experimental and experiential practice of Deep Listening. They are rather tools of a living practice (like "One Word", XII), passed and shaped from lip to lip, body to body, breath to breath, as a tissue of relationships.

It is not simply that the *Sonic Meditations* have acquired a body of scholarship or a tradition of practice, in the way that other texts (like this one!) change through interpretations that supplement and affect our understanding of them. Nor have these words altered just because times have changed such that we inevitably bring different experiences to bear on them. The paradoxical essence of these *Meditations* is that Oliveros used everyday words in the form of instructions, prompts, invitations, suggestions, and questions as catalysts for shared actions of *transformation* that affect both those who practice them and the words themselves. Approached with the discipline they encourage, they are *algorithmic and generative*.

One way to consider this is to contrast them with conventions of musical 'works'. This might also have the benefit of clarifying a little those queries or objections about whether they are music at all, or if they are rather a form of mindfulness or somatic practice (like tai chi).

Musical works are peculiar constructions. In the classical tradition, they simultaneously offer at least three different relations to time: the time (duration *and* historical moment) of performance, the era of composition, and perhaps—touching both—a moment of eternity or timelessness (the 'art'). Three in one, and sharing a similar implicit hierarchy to the Trinity of God the Father, Son, and Spirit; or the Idea, the Manifestation, and the Act.

The *Sonic Meditations* do not layer times in this way. The words refer us to seemingly commonplace actions like breathing or walking, not to a fixed model, score, or authoritative *Urtext*. Where music gives us a feeling for time and place—hits of the 1980s, say, or Mozart's Vienna—the *Sonic Meditations* do not 'belong' to late-1960s and early-1970s California. Nor are they 'timeless'. Rather, the eternal, like the feeling of weightlessness, defying gravity, is manifest only in this instant and as the act—as with "Teach[ing] Yourself to Fly". To repeat an exercise, especially daily, is not to perfect it in the sense of finding an identity with an 'original' that is always the same, but to incorporate its way of attending to time through your own unique qualities, those of others you are connecting with, and those of this very moment. *They are to be created in the fullest sense, not re-created.* To follow the words is to make them yours, without them becoming your property.

The *Sonic Meditations* are not musical works, then, but they are most definitely *musical*. Consider "Energy Changes" (XIII, also meditation XIX), acknowledging her experience with Elaine Summers' "kinetic awareness" (with its own threads weaving back to Elsa Gindler, a pioneer of women's group bodywork). Oliveros invites us to "listen to the environment as a drone" whilst simultaneously tuning inwards to sounds of our "blood pressure, heart beat and nervous system". These movements of "internal" attention and "external" awareness combine in one gesture—like a two-legged action—dimensions that are separated in John Cage's *4'33"*: his fabled account of hearing his own blood circulation and nervous system in an anechoic chamber (designed to cancel any external sounds or reverberation); and presentations of the work that feature the ambient environmental sounds of the situation. *4'33"* makes audible that there is no experience of pure silence; it also provides a novel experience of time through listening, a time that is not conditioned by expectation. "Energy Changes" takes this further by enacting our capacity to affect how we experience time —changing the field through focused listening—whilst letting ourselves be affected and changed by voluntarily opening to this global vibrating field of "Sonic Energy".

Oliveros notes that "music is a welcome by-product of this activity." In the same way, might our experience of being in time—of being fully alive—with others be a by-product of these exercises? She encourages us to experience ourselves as neither simply 'in' time—a time somehow external to us, in Greenwich perhaps—nor 'of' time, an internal clock and mental construct of self-narrative. Her musical wisdom equips those who listen deeply to centre themselves *as* time.

"Introduction II" outlines four features of the *Meditations* always in combination: sounding; imagining; listening; and remembering. Sounding and listening offer ways of relating to or addressing what for convenience we call 'the present'; imagining and remembering invoke resonances of 'the past' and 'the future'. Our passage through time involves ways of moving between these registers, both of which involve processes of externalising and internalising. Like walking ("Native", V), which requires one leg to receive the body's weight whilst the other pushes against gravity, our temporal 'posture' and 'balance' combines a constant double-movement between a voluntary process of letting time weigh and a wilful tension of making and shaping it, between recording all sounds indiscriminately into memory and of recalling them to the present. The *Sonic Meditations* are methods of research for each of us—together—to find our own ambulation, our gait, our musical phrasing.

If time courses like a river, then the waters of our day are increasingly turbulent, often polluted, running dry or spilling over their banks, flooding streets, and—without momentum—improvising stilled lakes. It does not have to be this way. Time is perhaps *the* issue now, characterized by many as combining simultaneously a sense of sublime and perilous acceleration *and* a feeling that nothing changes, that we are somehow stuck on repeat, a "presentism" (as François Hartog termed it) without futurity. Oliveros' *Sonic Meditations* offer us liquid tools to alter this. We do not return to them, ever the same, because we are not 'in' time that is external to us, sweeping us along in its current. They invite us to *be the flow*, to become timely through a disciplined listening. Incorporating them through daily exercises—learning again how to walk, to move, to breathe with others—we can find ourselves connected not only online but through telepathy, sympathetic resonance, imagination, remembrance, sounding, and listening.

"The music relates to the people who make it through participation and sharing, as a stream or river whose waters offer refreshment and cleansing to those who find it. What an extraordinary and beautiful promise. Can you hear it? Can you sound it?"

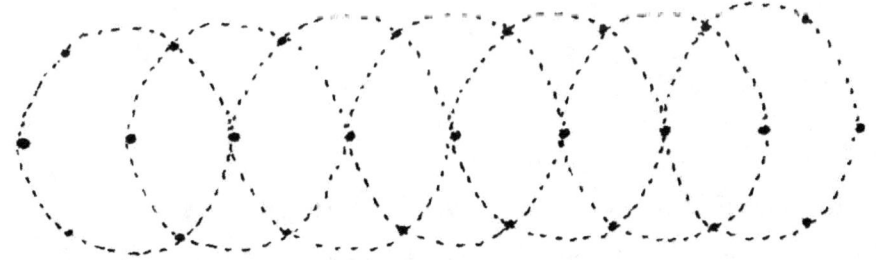

A Few Messages From Friends

"Taken together, the individual pieces that make up Pauline Oliveros's *Sonic Meditations* constitute one of the most vital and important scores since 1945. Oliveros puts not simply sound – the basic material of musicality – at the heart of each of meditation; she also calls for a mutual and acute practice of listening."

— Louise Gray, *The Wire*, London

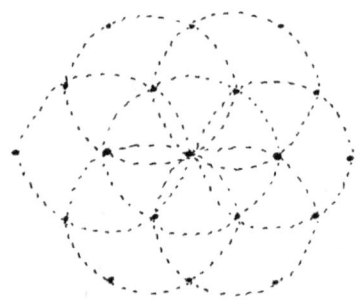

"In May 1971 Pauline wrote to me:

'We have organized an ensemble which is exclusively female.

We call ourselves the ♀ Ensemble ... Oh, the experience of communicating with women on this level is exhilarating and powerful. We are concentrating on Sonic Meditations at present .'

Over the next months she sent me meditations I - X, which an informal group of us in the UK explored and were ourselves exhilarated by all that we discovered and were learning. Then came a transatlantic stereo ESP event - an experiment in telepathic sonic meditation, which also involved Alvin Lucier and set up a lovely energy flow going across the Atlantic, as she wrote.

These were liberating, affirming explorations for us, as they have been for so many ever since those beginnings and I feel much gratitude to her. I also feel that they were culturally pivotal, returning us to a necessary awareness of sound's power to create community and to sustain us."

— Annea Lockwood

"Sonic Meditations is the foundation, the breathing, the voice that emerges, the tuning, the skin, the light touch, the rhythmical wink of the heart, the soft-wEAR of Deep Listening. It is the hidden passcODE to travel wirelessly to our forgotten deepest essence, and wonder again when we remember its soundings."

— Ximena Alarcón

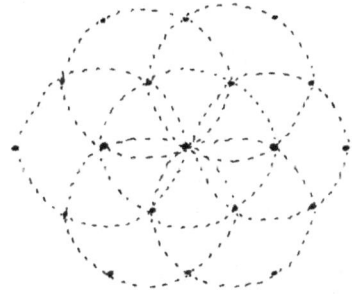

"It is 1976. A miracle occurs. Pauline's 'Sonic Meditations' land in my life.

Once per week I meet with friends. We partake in these radical offerings; the freedom to play; a quiet elegance takes over. Our bodies in resonance; every sound, every voice is important.

Then, I meet Pauline. Our interests intersect; another miracle! For 3 ½ decades I am at Pauline's side; always returning to this body of work; forever expanding resonance; deep nourishing peace."

— Heloise Gold

"I first encountered Pauline's Sonic Meditations in the 1980s as a student at UC Santa Cruz, where I eagerly sought out friends with whom I could explore the scores. After one session we were so completely relaxed and contented that we drifted off into dreamy sleep! I have since continued to enjoy Sonic Meditations as luminous—and sometimes enigmatic—portals to playful creativity and to vibrant, deeply listening community. Experiencing Sonic Meditations and Deep Listening has shown me that listening awareness is the wellspring of joy. "

— Jennifer Wilsey

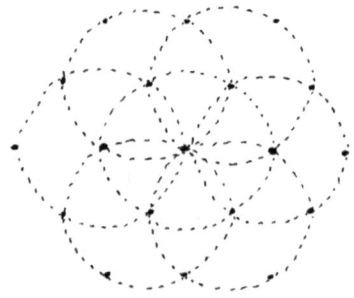

"Remembering sitting out on my fire escape ledge with Pauline, sipping herbal tea together when she was still a neighbor before moving upstate. And Pauline lying down on my couch while I played Music Mouse for her, which she had asked me to do. We can still savor memories at least, despite her absence. Pauline touched so many lives so beautifully!"

— Laurie Spiegel

EARTH TO SKY

a cave had no light yet letters sounded, and the future emanated

as walls

became

membrane (trembling)

emblems

of

earth and sky

\

INTERSPACE

INTERSPECTRAL

Bardo of becoming a

laboratory of conglomeration

a thin membrane

resonates with thin line of

thought

of echo

"what is the imprint of the musician mind?"

points to Medicine Buddha

(ascending vocal:
hold the light

hold....the .....night

(descending vocal:
hold the soil

old the oil

holding toil......turning the
coil.

what loop of time
held the lines

Medicine Buddha holding the myrobalan plant

and a begging bowl filled with healing nectar
deity seated on a thousand petalled lotus jeweled throne

Tay Ya Ta Om Be Kan Dze Be Kan Dze

Ma-ha Be Kan Dze Ra Dza Sa Mud Ga Te SO- HA

oMMMMMMMMMMMMM

Cave was

divination

Cave was ordinary mind

CAVE WAS ILLUSIVE

I STUDIED CAUVET

I STUDIED ITS TENDENCIES

I GAMBOLED WITH THE PSYCHE

OF FUTURE SOUND

I STUDIED ITS PROCLAMATION TO FUTURE SEEKERS

"I, PAULINE HAD EAR

I HAD SILENCE

I had will of the Human

drive

thrust to be heard

to be ensorcelled in the

gap of light and shadow

to be in conversation with...

the cave mind:

skull

the atrium

cathedral

tone poem

tomb poem

chorus crepuscular

the savage conversation

the peace of centuries sleeping

within the Permian

Cave was shouting

its sinecure

its sound

the earth had parted

the earth had crumbled

the earth had risen again

including cave

E Ma Ho"

Happy yogini

sanctuary where you find it

is inner ear

the shapes of animals coming through

and earth is a willow, earth is

what had entered

with wind

with lived consciousness

rays from what source?

they –spelunkers -- made out

"nymphs with partridges wear the order of the swan"

then

"an alchemy of nudity and animalia and honor"

they marveled as string theory

metastasized with more dark energy

they said, cave: is this it--

hope and fear?

how may I tread lightly here?

as tentacular directions in the

multiverse reveal themselves

cave was sanctuary was laboratory was seclusion

"time and space are always ambiguous"

but we knew that, they said

"& turbulent, terrifying"

TURRRRRRRRRRRR

BUUUUUUU

LENTTTTTTTTTTTTTT

an elixir shot in the arm, vision of bandaged angel-mouth

our world our world, night's solipsistic bubble!

this is Fra Angelico at our beckoning
this is tongue of the votary

the aficionado

the listener

the

blindfolded deity on cave wall

art & meditation wrestling in a gold rimmed universe
and at its center, a death mask, tongue with heavy chain

Oracle: didn't hear it coming, a dark plague year
born of a bat on another turf's shadow

didn't see the affinity

& staying inside the discos so long....

this is a new world, another axis

not enough elucidation not enough
evolutional topical optimization of vibrating continuum
to reckon, bond, tie, link

meanwhile "firmaments"

"dangle easy" and scare

an imaginary continuous present
where nomadic talismans open like hands
like wings like lips likes shards on the path
cuneiform inscribed with amity, praise, poetry
the poets say *love in every part of the world*
will know the myth of this time

its lessons of sorrows

"this angle of sunlight is the key, please supplicate the AI angel
who'll guide us to gnosis warm and settled"

[The AI Angel is in training,

the earth heaves in plague time

the skies will bind the light of this time, this time

say it again: this time this time]

Tay Ya Ta ,   Om Be Kan Dze,   Be Kan DZE

— Anne Waldman: Text for Pauline Oliveros performance Dec 11. 2021
With sound improvisation by Nathan Wheeler

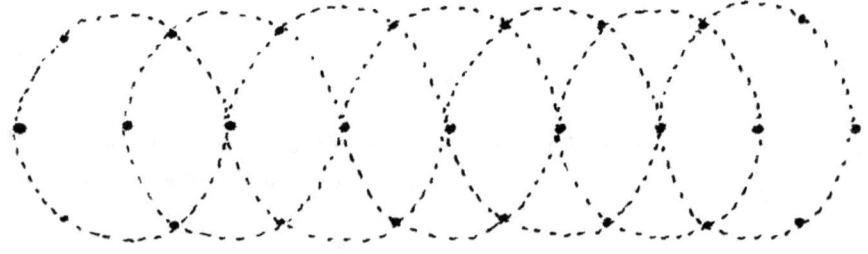

Pauline Oliveros (1932-2016) Pauline Oliveros' life as a composer, performer and humanitarian was about opening her own and others' sensibilities to the universe and facets of sounds. Her career spanned fifty years of boundary dissolving music making. In the '50s she was part of a circle of iconoclastic composers, artists, poets gathered together in San Francisco. In the 1960's she influenced American music profoundly through her inclusive work with improvisation, meditation, electronic music, myth and ritual. The recipient of four Honorary Doctorates, and, among her many recent awards, the William Schuman Award for Lifetime Achievement, Columbia University, New York, NY; The Giga-Hertz-Award for Lifetime Achievement in Electronic Music from ZKM, Center for Art and Media, Karlsruhe, Germany; and The John Cage award from from the Foundation of Contemporary Arts. Oliveros was Distinguished Research Professor of Music at Rensselaer Polytechnic Institute, Troy, NY, and Darius Milhaud Artist-in-Residence at Mills College. She founded 'Deep Listening®,' which came from her childhood fascination with sounds and from her works in concert music with composition, improvisation and electro-acoustics. She described Deep Listening as a way of listening in every possible way to everything possible to hear no matter what you are doing. Such intense listening includes the sounds of daily life, of nature, of one's own thoughts as well as musical sounds. 'Deep Listening is my life practice,' Oliveros explained, simply. Oliveros founded Deep Listening Institute, formerly Pauline Oliveros Foundation, now the Center For Deep Listening at Rensselaer, NY. Her creative work is currently disseminated through Pauline Oliveros Publications and the Ministry of Maåt, Inc

paulineoliveros.us

'Through Pauline Oliveros and Deep Listening, I finally know what harmony is...It's about the pleasure of making music.'

— John Cage.

pop & mom

www.ingramcontent.com/pod-product-compliance
Lightning Source LLC
Chambersburg PA
CBHW050449010526
44118CB00013B/1746